WHAT'S LEFT

ALSO BY SUSAN READ CRONIN

POETRY

Notices

OPEN

CHILDREN'S BOOKS

The Magician's Assistant

NON-FICTION

Bronze Casting in a Nutshell

WHAT'S LEFT

Susan Read Cronin

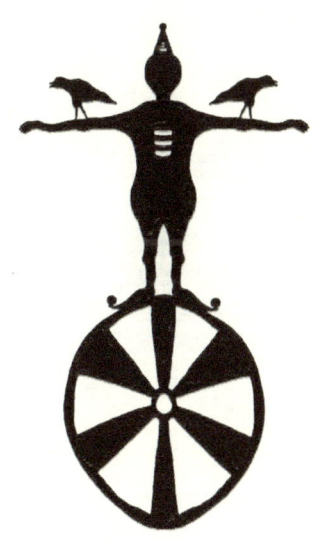

Suzo Media, Santa Barbara
2022

Copyright © 2022 Susan Read Cronin

All rights reserved. No part of this book may be reproduced
or used in any manner without the prior written permission
of the copyright owner, except for the use of brief quotations in a book review.

To request permissions, contact the publisher at SuzoMediaCo@gmail.com

ISBN: 978-1-7350460-9-9

Library of Congress Control Number: 2022916369

First paperback edition 2022

Book design by Chryss Yost
Cover art by Susan Read Cronin

Suzo Media
281 Hot Springs Road
Montecito, CA 93108

www.SusanReadCronin.com

TABLE OF CONTENTS

The Fire

The Undertaker Says, *Feel Free*	15
Shadow	16
Face the World	17
Nothing to Hold	18
Walking Home	19
The Fire	20
Out for Repair	22
Her Big Idea	23
Secret Wedding	24
Unborn	25
On the Dirt Road in Front of the Gunsmith's House	26
The Rose	27
On the Way to JFK	28
Notes to Self	32
John Doe	34

Just B.

The Executor	41
A Veteran	43
Playing Doctor	44
Just B.	45

Harboring Resentments	47
When No One Is Watching	48
The Purple Orchid	49
Scared Shitless at Seventeen	50
Knock! Knock! Guess Who?	53
Journey to the Center of the Earth	54
If You Ask Me	56
Do You Want Me	57
ESL	58
Falling in Love	59
Thinking of You	60
Happy Birthday! She Cries Out	62

LEFT

A Labor of Love	69
Stand In	70
Love in the Time of LGBTQ	71
William Tell's Daughter	72
It's About the Oak Tree Outside Our House—	74
Fear of Falling	76
In Harmony	77
Left	79
Dance Inside My Head	80

The Four Stages of *I Don't Want To*	81
Hansel and Gretel	82
One Last Breath	83
I Stopped by Your Grave Today, Dad	84
Once Upon a Time	85
Notes	88
Acknowledgements	89
Dedications	90
About the Author	91

For The Old Belgian

THE FIRE

They left a mess—me in ruins.

The Undertaker Says, *Feel Free*

to stay as long as you like. He escorts
my mother and me, past a pile of
raked leaves, to the carriage house
—the crematorium—

to see Dad

lying there in his chosen cardboard coffin—
blue flannel pajama bottoms, no top—
suiting him just fine, just as he had wanted.

His eyes are closed—his face like a baby bird's
before his feathers grow in—mouth open wide,
waiting for his mother to return with food.

Mom smooths his forehead, plants a kiss there,
tells him that she loves him as she lays her hands
on top of his. Four hands, like folded wings.

Mourning doves lament outside while I stand here—
feel my pain—wish *she* had been the first to go.

SHADOW

How it waddles before me—

this shadow, the shape of it—

it's my mother, for sure.

In mirrors, sometimes,

her face shows up in mine

—that mouth & chin—

but never have I seen

her on the ground before—

grabbing my shadow.

FACE THE WORLD

Oh, bad late-night habits, says the mirror—

judges the shadows below my eyes. In my face—

fair, square, it doesn't show my inner world,

where only I know what in the world

I think, or say to myself in that mirror,

as I gaze kindly upon my face, that face

that's grown on me. I turn, face

the day—greet the outside world.

People call out to me, *Mirror!*

Mirror—to my face—*Reflect the world back to us!*

NOTHING TO HOLD

When an astronaut cries in space

    his tears float off his face.

Will my tears float away

    the same way, too, when

you are gone—there being nothing

    left to hold them here?

WALKING HOME

I hear sirens close by—firetrucks
roar up my street: whose house is it?
I follow a hose from the hydrant
to our house—Oh *fuck*—

the fire crews are in *our* yard,
run lines to our pond,
suck out thousands of gallons—
pump them on our roof.

You're lucky, the fire chief says.
We made it just in time. Am I lucky?

Yes, I guess, I say and watch over
his shoulder the moon begin to rise.

THE FIRE

What got me wasn't so much the smell
of burnt wood, smoke, wet wool, and plaster,
but the invasion—fifty firemen in heavy gear,
tramping through our home.

When they got to my bedroom, did they see
my underwear? Why did I feel so hot with shame
as I stood outside and watched? They were there
to save our house. They left a mess—me, in ruins.

For weeks, men I don't recognize come up to me—
proudly—tell me *they* put the fire out.
I'm so grateful, I say and then burn myself out—

spending days wrestling with adjusters,
dry cleaners, contractors, the need to pack
and repack, take inventory, sort and stack.

Winter, when we move back in, the house
off-gassing fresh paint and urethane,
propane flames flicker in the fireplace
where hand-split logs once burned.

I use my cast iron frying pan to make our first meal—
onions, garlic, and lots of greasy sausage that burst
and spray their spittle at me. Their rich aroma lines
the pockets of our house with the smell of home again.

OUT FOR REPAIR

My black suede shoes look
down and out. Seen better days.

More times than I can count, they
carry this portly package out the door.

And what have I given them in return
for their years of saddled servitude?

A quick brush here. A wipe there.
I brought them to get resoled—

how I miss them—my beasts of burden—
they need no halter, no reins—

my black suede schleppers,
to carry me home again.

HER BIG IDEA

It was my mother who asked
you to marry me. Remember?

Kathmandu was her big idea—
so she could go trekking in Nepal.

1976. Remember? I had to dress
her on my wedding day, as if she

were the bride. I wanted to cry—
instead, I stuffed my feet into

my shoes. They were blue.

What was I getting into?
What if I didn't say, *I do?*

But then I did—and here
I am still with you.

SECRET WEDDING

We stood and said our vows deep

in the pines of northern Vermont.

November snow sifted through the boughs,

covering the hood and wetting the shoulders

of my black wool cape.

We said *I do*

as everything turned white like the icing

on the sheet cake that waited for us inside.

We cut the cake, shared it with our two

witnesses and the Justice of the Peace,

a stranger, whom we never saw again.

Unborn

      small person,
you move inside me.

      I am a piñata.
You are the prize.

ON THE DIRT ROAD IN FRONT OF THE GUNSMITH'S HOUSE

I don't think I could go through that,

I tell Sally at the end of her driveway.

I'm standing here sweating, swatting

at a swarm of black flies, circling

my head—maybe I'm making it worse.

She, in her blue house dress:
I'd do it all over again. God gave me
five years with her. She was a gift.
How to love—that's what I learned.

She sets purple petunias, tenderly,

in a bald truck tire, filled with dirt.

I'm so sad for you, Sally.

I'm newly pregnant—only 24.

If I knew, like her, I would lose

this child, would I go ahead and have it?

THE ROSE

The rose does not sit in its bud vase and complain

that last night it did not sleep well or that it is feeling old.

It unfurls before me—pink petals pull back to reveal the gold

the bees like but can't get to here, inside, at my kitchen table.

ON THE WAY TO JFK

The couple behind us has been bickering
non-stop since we boarded the plane in Athens.

An announcement in Greek—passengers gasp.
Rosaries fly in the sky above some seats.
I hear prayers in a language I do not know.

35,000 feet above the Atlantic, I watch
> the plane icon
> on the map
> on the wall
> in the front
> of the cabin
> turn back
> head back
> east towards
> Ireland.

The same announcement comes on in English now:
There's a   threat of a bomb   in the cargo area.
We're headed   to land   to Shannon.

Silence, swollen on recycled air, finally forces
the couple behind us to shut the fuck up.

I take my husband's hand,
say, *We've had a good life.
I love you*—he says, *Yes—
we've been so lucky.* Yes, I say.
Maybe this, too, is luck? A gift—
to go together.

***

All eyes are forward on that map—
     plane icon
     headed east,
     backtracking
     across blue
     towards green—
     a clock
     on the screen
     ticks down
     the hour
     left to go.

Given time to wonder, I do—
Will it be a violent end? Torn to shreds?
Will the shock of ice-cold air deaden me
to sleep? Will I wake to some new place?

***

We land in Shannon's furthest field.
Relief sighs break the silence. But we're not done yet.
Fire trucks and foam sprayers surround us.

No need for escape chutes—we're orderly—
single file down the stairs, move quickly
to distant buses that take us to the terminal
two miles away, where there's no food
and we sleep on the cold polished floor
until dawn.

The *All Clear* comes and they load us
back on buses, back to the same plane.

***

Are we different people now
back in these same seats?
Grateful to have another day?

I know I am.

I take my husband's hand,
and as I look into his eyes,

I hear the couple behind our seat
pick up their fight again,
right where they left off.

NOTES TO SELF

Dear Susie,

Did you not get my memo?
Drop the sie.

Stop calling yourself Susie–
like a French poodle.

Grow up. It's time for you
to be a Susan.

And don't think having long hair makes you
look like you have more than you do.

It doesn't.

Susan

Dear Susan,

Thanks for your note.
You might be right—

maybe it is time for me to change
my name and bob my hair.

But time to grow up?
Never. Perhaps

it's time for you to stop
taking things so

seriously.

Susie

JOHN DOE

It's about John Doe.
Do you know him?

I can't find him
in the phonebook
or on Facebook,

but there he is—
in the morgue,
with a tag on his toe.

JUST B.

I wanted to be part of the crowd—
not stand out from it.

THE EXECUTOR

*Come by the house and pick out anything
you want,* the brother tells his sister
after their mother's death.

That Saturday, she finds him there.
Take anything you want, he says, sweeping
generous arms around the living room,
where she notices one of the two things
she had been thinking of—

her favorite lamp—a sextant on a marble base,
brass fittings and a green shade.

Her brother follows close behind, lets drop,
*There's just one thing that means
the world to me—it's that sextant lamp.
Anything but that.*

She moves to another part of the room—
towards the wooden desk she's always loved.

Her brother's voice seeps in her ear,

The campaign desk, well–
I've promised that to John.
How about a Windsor chair?

Does she really need any of this

stuff? It's not worth a fight.

Let him have it.

She goes down to the basement,

turns on the light, and there's

something she really wants—

an old grenade, glued to a piece of wood.

The number 1, printed on a metal tag, hangs

from its unpulled pin. A plaque below it reads:

> COMPLAINT DEPARTMENT
> Please Take a Number

She hasn't realized he's followed her

down the stairs. *I don't need that*, he says.

You can have it.

A VETERAN

Going home, home, soon he'll be going home—
unsent letters in his chest pocket, written in blood,
leak their ink, drench his core. How this war

has worn him down. And inside him, yet another war—
sorrow unravels the knitted socks, sent from home,
that strain to keep him warm in this trench of blood

that stains his boots, soaks his soul with the blood
running from his brothers, slain in this wretched war—
running from the enemy, unseen. He will return home,

silent—home, he will go alone, blood-letted by this war.

PLAYING DOCTOR

I went to play at Jimmy's house.
We hid in an attic room where

we stripped down. He showed me
his. I showed him mine.

His brother peeped through
the keyhole and yelled—

*Mommy! Susie and Jimmy
are playing doctor!*

Head hanging in shame,
I was sent home—

Bad! Bad! Bad!
What became of us?

I went into the creative arts.
Jimmy? He's a coroner now.

JUST B.

Lucky them! The parents with kids called
Cameron or Kate—they can buy personalized
mugs and magnets at the souvenir shop
here on Fisherman's Wharf.

I don't see one of the names given
to my own children or grandchildren,
and I feel sad to have to settle for a generic
postcard or a bag of saltwater taffy for them.

But there—there's *my* name—embossed
on a mini license plate—*my* name, so popular,
there were three of us in my class at school.
They told us apart by calling us
Susie, Susan, and Sue.

My sister and brother were named after family
members—middle names included. Me?
I got a name found at the bottom of the S page
in the 1950's *What to Name Your Baby* book.
No middle name, just the initial *B*.

In first grade, they asked me,
What's your middle name?
B, I said.
Like a bumble bee? they asked.
No, I said. B, like the letter B.
That's not a name, they said—
that doesn't count.

When I cried, my parents said, *Be grateful*
 to stand out from the crowd—like Susan B. Anthony.

Susan B. who? I didn't care. I just wanted
to fit in—in my family, in my class, at school.
I wanted to be part of the crowd—
not stand out from it.

Over six decades later, here on this wharf,
looking at my name in the throng of personalized
nick-nacks in the morass of a souvenir shop,
did I stand out or did I fit in?

What I wanted all along was to be comfortable
in my own skin—to know I can just be—
just B.

HARBORING RESENTMENTS

Bobbing in the bay,

tied up to buoys,

little white dinghies—

transoms emblazoned

> *Life Insurance*
> *Liars and Cheats*
> *Thinning Hair*
> *Great Expectations*

None worth clinging to.

WHEN NO ONE IS WATCHING

I stroke my bed, whisper—

how lucky am I?

I dance naked, fist-pump—

jump in the air—say, *Yes!*

I pick roses, strip their leaves,

snip the tips off their thorns.

When no one is watching

I write *You are loved* on a paper

towel in the middle of the stack.

I stare at the back of

men's necks—will them to

turn around.

When no one is watching?

That's when I want to be seen.

THE PURPLE ORCHID

To think I'd planned to give you away.

Your purple just doesn't fit here—
anywhere. I need my plants to match
my décor—so sue me.

When our guests brought you as a gift last night,
I graciously accepted you and hid a sigh
behind my smile—who can I give *this* one to?

I reserve the right to change my mind

as I watch the light settle on your velvet blooms,
and see inside your flowers' rooms, small-beaked birds
feeding their young in nests rimmed in cobalt blue.

And when I view you from behind, iridescent blue
butterflies cling to your one long stem,
as if they'll pull you from your pot.

No, stay! Come with me upstairs—to my room—
to a spot where the light is just right.

SCARED SHITLESS AT SEVENTEEN

Sitting alone in the doctor's waiting room,
I'm sure—it's cancer. Definitely melanoma.

I've been scared to touch the spot on my neck
for a week—ever since my mother said, *Oh, God,
what's that? You need to go to the doctor!*

Hyperpigmentation, he declares, after close
examination of that hollow between
my collarbones. He presses a prescription
in my hand: *Use this cream twice a day.*

Shaky, in front of my mirror, gingerly,
lightly, ever so carefully, with a dab of cream
on my finger, I circle the spot.

Gently, ever so gently, I rub it in:
brown lilliputian rice granules appear—
so tiny—

My heart quickens a beat.

My skin! It's peeling off!

Oh my God!

It's not my skin, it's—

                      dirt.

HOW HANSEL AND GRETEL AFFECTED MY HOUSEKEEPING SKILLS AS A CHILD

    I was the one who always cleared
    the table at the end of the meal—

    shook the placemats, swept *all*
    the crumbs into my cupped hand—

    and sprinkled them behind me
    in a trail on the way to the kitchen

    to ask

    how

    else

    I could

    help—

KNOCK! KNOCK! GUESS WHO?

White pebbles
Stale breadcrumbs
A rusty bird cage
A chicken bone

Four kidney-shaped dried beans
A sway-backed cow
Large waxy green leaves
A giant golden goose egg

A swatch of red wool
The corner of a wicker picnic basket
Broken wire-rimmed glasses frames
A set of fangs

1. Hansel 2. Jack 3. The Wolf

JOURNEY TO THE CENTER OF THE EARTH

Get your PJ's on, pronto!
Mummy announces after
spaghetti and meatballs.
Tonight, we're going to the movies.

The movies? We've never been!

I pull on my PJ's, the pink ones,
grab my slippers, slide down
the banister and run to the car.

Daddy drives like the devil—
Mummy, in front, as excited
as the three of us in the back,
sliding loose around the corners.

*Mummy, why do we have to
wear pajamas to the movies?*

That's what all kids do.
And you'll be ready for bed
when we get home!

The marquee is all lit up—

Journey to the Center of the Earth,
Daddy reads out as we go in.

Smell of popcorn in the lobby,
grown-ups nod their heads our way,
smile. We smile back, notice
other children there too—

none of them in pajamas.
Not a one.

IF YOU ASK ME

I'll tell you I love avocados

I'll warn you not to get too close

I'll let you know how I feel if I feel like it

I'll think about it

I'll share my dislike for Old Spice

I'll reveal my 7th grade crush

I'll expose my scar

I'll instruct you how to hold a fork correctly

I'll say my name in Japanese

I'll tell on you

I'll voice my opinion

I'll divulge I read *The National Enquirer*

I'll throw spaghetti at the wall

I'll re-count the times you forgot

I'll deny I had an affair

I'll advise you not to be so nosy

I'll declare I didn't do it

I'll ask *you*, "Why do you ask?"

Do You Want Me

                to tell you
food is stuck between your teeth,
there's ketchup on your cheek
and lettuce in your lap?

Not all at once, mind you—

would I let you know if your shirt is
buttoned wrong or your fly is down.

Want me whisper to you when
your comb-over's come unglued?

Would you mind if I let you know?
You wouldn't mind, would you?

Don't mind if I do.

ESL

She would have
She could have
She should have
left him

but

She wouldn't
She couldn't
She didn't

Her heart wouldn't
let her

FALLING IN LOVE

It's such a heart-racing,
clock-stopping time!

Tick Tock!
Let's lock lips!

I could fall in love with you,
or you—even you!

What if I could fall
back in love with me?

Thinking of You

in a restaurant—I wipe the sauce
off my lips, go to wash my hands.

There lies a pile of the smooth paper
towels, the ones you love so much.

Thinking of you, I slide a handful
inside the lining of my blue down coat.

Again, no one catches me stealing—
this time in Chicago—those soft
paper towels from a fancy club

as I think of you—the temptation
too great, my pockets too deep.

Are paper towel grabs a gateway to much worse?

At a wedding luncheon, a linen
napkin drapes my lap—I slap my hand,

say, *No!* No more pilfering, even if

it is for you, my friend. My dearest,

will you forgive me? But maybe

there is no need for forgiveness,

for what you wanted is not what

I lay before you now—

how did I not see this before?

You only wanted me,

                          thinking of you.

Happy Birthday! She Cries Out

    as I walk by her on the beach—this tall, black,
    beautiful woman in a blue spandex body suit

    doing deep knee bends, smiling right at me.
    Today is my birthday. How did she know?

    I smile back. Do I know her? Do I?
    No, never seen her before.

    My steps spring into the tide's cold waves
    that wash the sand and the soles of my feet.

    Must be that happy birthday aura around me
    she notices. Happy,
                    yes,
                              happy,
                                        I wave.
                                                  She nods

    and adjusts her left earbud—continues to talk
    to the person she's been talking to all along

    on her phone—the person who is celebrating
    their birthday today.

LEFT

If I left, there would be no one
left on the left, right?

A LABOR OF LOVE

You're making breakfast? Great!
I'll have two fried eggs and toast.

Eggs? Second shelf down—no—
to your left. That's right.

No, I didn't hide the butter—
it's in the fridge door.

The frying pan?
Center drawer.

One piece of toast is fine. Uh-huh—
turn the knob to the right—

that's right—right. Uh-huh—

STAND IN

She allows his touch—wants it to be
just for her, not for all his past lovers

who may have looked like her,
smelled like her, moved like her.

Does he even see her?

He had a lifetime of touches
before she met him—she knows—

yet he doesn't want to know of her
earlier lovers—nothing of her past:

she is the driven snow—the clean, crisp
sheet stretched on the hotel room bed.

She wants to know—is she the only one now?
She, the one standing in front of him?

Should she allow his touch?
Could it be meant for someone else.

She wants to know.
She fears the answer.

LOVE IN THE TIME OF LGBTQ

She loves her—

she loves her not.

He loves him—

he loves him not.

They love them—

they love them not.

I love you—

I love you not.

Poor Daisy—

you need more petals.

William Tell's Daughter

    stands still, facing him,
    her shining face as round as

    the apple—

    Sir Isaac Newton watches
    drop from the same tree

    Eve plucks the fruit from
    to hand to Adam, who takes

    a bite—

    that causes Snow White to lie
    motionless until awakened by

    a kiss—

    a kiss so powerful, it shoots
    round the world,

plants itself on the dimpled

cheek of William Tell's daughter,

as she stands still and waits for him

to pull back the string of his bow.

It's About the Oak Tree Outside Our House—

a battalion of caterpillars stripped every single

leaf, then repelled down sticky strings

to the ground, where no bird dared eat them.

Green soldiers, crawling on their bellies

across the open battlefield of gravel driveway,

they make it to our home—scale the stucco walls.

At dawn, a million moths now shade the sky,

circle the oak's carcass, wiry branches stiff like

the new hair on my sister's scalp after chemo—

how often does a body need to fight a war

not of its own making? I have no answer.

Dust-colored swarms assemble, fly

in formation towards our house.

What orders them to beat

against our panes?

Late afternoon, outside, a woman marvels—

Oh! How lovely! So many butterflies—

her arms raised to the sky,

where the sinking sun casts its bladed rays

against the oak—its long shadow a lace skeleton.

Fear of Falling

                hair—

                        the crop

                                  uproots—

            parachutes

                                        to the ground.

Birds will find it—

                weave it

                                    in their nests—

to keep their babies'

                bums warm.

IN HARMONY

I'm sure it's an aging rock star
at the table across from us.

He has all the signs—long, dyed,
black hair, shirt with head-spinning

designs—pants' zippers everywhere—
fancy shit-kicking boots.

But there's a softness about his face.
He looks at me. I glance just past

his head—catch him in my periphery.
This is a town where one does not gawk.

Does he think I'm hot? I'm not
twenty-five anymore, but then neither

is he. He continues to look my way,
which is more than young salesgirls do,

when I signal for help. I give him
a slight nod. I know it's not my body—

it's not hot—I'm a grand-mère,
with white hair wearing Crocs.

I go home and google a bit
to find his image—and there he is,

rocking his guitar at a nursing home,
leading a sing-along with the inmates.

Maybe someday I'll be singing
along with him in harmony.

LEFT

When I left the room,

there were two people left—

one on the right,

one on the left.

The one on the right

turned to the one on the left

and said, *I thought
you'd already left.*

No, he replied.
*If I left, there would be
no one left on the left,
right?*

Then, leaving what

to do next up to

the one on the right,

he left.

DANCE INSIDE MY HEAD

Without arms or legs
    how can light foxtrot
        into the room

and shoeless ideas
    dance inside my head?
        Waltz, tango, two-step,

sliding towards me
    looking, looking
        for a partner.

THE FOUR STAGES OF *I DON'T WANT TO*

AGE 5: If I don't want to go to swimming lessons—

I run around my room in a tight circle,
stare at a lightbulb until my face turns red,
then stagger from my room saying, *I don't feel so well.*

AGE 25: If I don't want to go to a party—

I thank the hosts, tell them, *I so want to go,
but I'm feeling under the weather—wouldn't want
to spread whatever it is I have.*

AGE 50: If I don't want to go to Italy with a group—

I tell them, *I love the Italians! Their food! The art!
Oh, darn, those dates. Sorry, it won't work out.*

AGE NOW: If there is anything I don't want to do—

I stay home and say, *Fuck it!*

HANSEL AND GRETEL

Hansel!

Open the cage! Leave
that chicken bone
behind! Pluck all
the candy!
Stuff your pockets!
Come! Run!
Help me!
The gingerbread!
Crumble it!
Trail it behind us!
Quick! Run!

Gretel—

the crumbs are

all gone—

we can leave

no trail. Here—

take my hand—

laugh with me

at the birds eating

scraps of ash

along the way—

along this long

long way to Hell.

ONE LAST BREATH

Every year my breath blows out
the candles on store-bought cakes.
And on each birthday: *Be polite*. Suck it up.

Suck in my breath, suck in my stomach.
Don't show how uncomfortable it is to be
the center of attention. Yet I crave it.

When I turn seven, I'm taught to hold back.
Let others have some cake first. Let them
play with my presents. Do as I am told.

On my 40th, my mother wants to come
on my family trip to her dream destination.
Our first day there we swear: *Never again*.

Now she's gone. Have I missed her? No. But
yes. Maybe. She gave me birth after all.

Breathe in. Breathe out.

I STOPPED BY YOUR GRAVE TODAY, DAD

I see Betty's been by, added to her scattered shrine
of junk. No doubt she means well. Who am I

to judge the plastic snowman angled in a bucket
of weeds? *For God's sake! It's summer now!*

At least she got the solar flamingo right—it will glow
by Sandra's grave—keep you company at night.

And she's placed a pair of pigs on spikes to dance for Pat—
one has lost its head. Sad. Maybe you like it this way—

windchimes tinkling throughout the day,
fake flowers fading on their stalks?

Who am I to say? I'm just passing through.

I used to be the one who tended to things—
now I tend to forget. So forgive me, Dad,

maybe I best let Betty take it from here.

Once Upon a Time

there was a

giant

princess

witch

fairy

ogre

wood cutter

toy soldier

who lived

in a castle

in the trunk of a tree

in a house in the woods

under a bridge

in a cave

in a match box

on a cloud.

Every day, he/she/they would

sit and weep

cast spells

flit about

say *Fe Fi Fo Fum*

march around in circles

chop wood

eat candy

until there was nothing left.
Nothing.

NOTES

Herein, I write the usual disclaimer to say that (most) names have been changed. If you think I am writing about you, you're right. But then so few people read poetry, odds are good I'll get away with it.

I apologize to you, dear reader, if you are offended by my use of the word *fuck*: in "The Fire" (page 20)—I had to rhyme something with "firetrucks"; in "On the Way to JFK" (page 28) and in "The Four Stages of *I Don't Want To*" (page 79) it was needed for some serious tonal emphasis.

"If You Ask Me", (page 56) enough time has gone by that I can now reveal the name of my seventh-grade crush—David Reid. I was partial to my last name and enjoyed thinking I wouldn't have to change it (other than its spelling) when we got married (which we didn't).

For those of you who grew up reading fairytales, you know the answers to "Knock! Knock! Guess Who?" (page 53). For those of you who didn't, it's never too late. You can find the Cliffs Notes versions in the last poem of this book, "Once Upon a Time" (page 85). This poem also appeared in my book OPEN (© Susan Read Cronin, 2021) so it's been used twice upon a time.

You may think I have a thing about Hansel and Gretel. I do.

ACKNOWLEDGEMENTS

To Ted, who continues to say, *Yes!* in answer to: *Want to hear a poem?* Such love, support and enthusiasm sustain me.

Thank you, Wright, for inspiring me with your wisdom and your favorite poets.

To Read, who finds the sword mightier than the pen. Keep that anvil ringing.

I am indebted to my dear friends' ears, in particular, those of Marilee Zdenek, Karin Muller, and Sas Carey.

To Laure-Anne Bosselaar—I am in awe of not only your ears, but your inky pen, your penchant for taking me to court, your help with revisions, your sense of humor, your intelligence, and all that wonderful *je ne sais quoi* that makes you who you are. With appreciation and gratitude, I thank you for letting me sit at your feet.

And to you, dear reader, for picking up this book and getting this far. Thank you.

DEDICATIONS

"Unborn" is dedicated to Read and Wright Cronin.

"On the Way to JFK" is for Ted Cronin.

"Just B." is for Teddy Lilly Cronin.

"How Hansel and Gretel Affected My Housekeeping Skills as a Child" is for Saffron Dove Cronin.

"Knock! Knock! Guess Who?" is for Misha Bean Cronin.

"Thinking of You" is for The Old Belgian.

ABOUT THE AUTHOR

How was I to know I would create a controversy at age four at Christ Church Nursery School when I painted the sun? Brush loaded with yellow, I aimed for the manilla paper, started with a large circle, filled in two dots for eyes, made a sweeping stroke for the mouth, a nose of a triangle, and radiant lines to the edges of the paper.

I was the second child of three my parents had in three years. All our names started with an S. On Parents' Day, I was proud that my mother was the youngest parent in the classroom. My father never came to school, as he was working.

I grew up in Mill Neck, on Long Island, in a 1700's house that sat on a bluff overlooking the Sound. In my room, I had a display of folk dolls but it was the baby dolls that got all my attention. One night, before tucking in with my favorite, I got a pair of scissors and cut its hair—sure it would grow back. It didn't.

My father would give us a quarter every time we noticed when he'd had a haircut. Every day, he took the train into the city, where he had a seat on the New York Stock Exchange. I imagined that he sold socks and stockings from a large drawer at the base of his throne.

He was a handsome hockey star and a freshman at Yale when he met my mother walking her goat to the beach. She was seventeen. That fall, he was kicked out—too much hockey and poker. After a stint in the Marines, he reapplied to Yale and asked my mother to marry him. He was successful on both counts.

My mother was born in New York City and raised mostly by household help. Her father was a famous financier who had a house in the city, two on Long Island, and one in the Bahamas. My mother, the youngest of three, claimed to be her father's favorite. Her mother called her her "Ugly Duckling."

At the age of seven, my mother developed an eye disease. Doctors injected her with typhoid in hopes of curing the problem. It didn't. She was sent to the Bahamian heat where she got to swim daily in the ocean on her father's back. He died suddenly the year after that. Throughout her life, she continued to be a great swimmer and blind in her right eye.

My father got home from work every night around 7. "Draw me a princess!" were the first words out of my mouth as I jumped on him. Having spent lots of time at college sketching in the margins of his notebooks, cartoons were his specialty. He drew announcement cards, Christmas cards, birthday cards, and published a few illustrated books.

In 1968 , I went away to boarding school and discovered creative writing. I wrote an illustrated autobiography in which I was a blue car. I peppered the school newspaper with articles and illustrations. Senior year, I was the editor. As my acceptance reply to Williams College to join their first class of women in 1971, I sent a watercolor cartoon of a girl in a school uniform carrying a suitcase running towards a sign with an arrow that said *Williams*.

I decided to be an English major. Halfway through sophomore year, bleary-eyed from having to read Moby Dick in a week and write a fifteen-page paper, I needed to find classes that had no reading and no term papers. Studio Art! I sketched, etched, I taught myself to sew. I made sculptures and published illustrations in the literary magazine.

My life has turned out to be a happy confluence of playing in both fields—art and language. I see things differently, like the sun I painted in nursery school. That day, I was the only one who had painted a nose on the sun. The other kids made fun of me. "The sun doesn't have a nose!"

"*Yes, it does!*"

"No, it doesn't!" said the chorus.

"*Yes, it does!*"

I was willing to go to the mat. Instead, the teacher made me wait on a bench by the door until my mother picked me up.

www.ingramcontent.com/pod-product-compliance
Lightning Source LLC
Chambersburg PA
CBHW020545080526
44583CB00013B/1003